The Book *of* Totality

Yun Wang

salmonpoetry

Published in 2015 by
Salmon Poetry
Cliffs of Moher, County Clare, Ireland
Website: www.salmonpoetry.com
Email: info@salmonpoetry.com

ISBN 978-1-910669-13-6

COVER ARTWORK: Susan Sheppard, West Virginia poet and artist. Oil on canvas.
COVER DESIGN & TYPESETTING: *Siobhán Hutson*
Printed in Ireland by Sprint Print

For my son Sam

Acknowledgments

Yun Wang gratefully acknowledges the following periodicals in which these poems, sometimes in earlier versions, first appeared:

The American Poetry Journal: "Dark Energy"
Apple Valley Review: "Adagio", "The Aggregate of Routines", "Echoes of Trees on the Mountaintop"
Blood Lotus: "The Poet and the Monkey"
Blue Fifth Review: "Meditation on Hair"
Boxcar Poetry Review: "Space Journal: Passage"
Chinese Literature Today: "Buffalo Point", "Space Journal: Time Machine", "Black Horse"
Cimarron Review: "The Elder Beauty", "Aspen Trees"
Diode: "Three Lotus Ponds", "Evolution"
FutureCycle Poetry: "Futurescape", "Dreamscape"
Janus Head: "Shard", "Whispers", "Condensation", "Transmutation in the Train", "Mirages of Indiscretion", "The Knot", "To the Alien Listening Through the Galactic Wormhole", "Conception", "Total Solar Eclipse"
Other Voices International: "Autumn", "The Gift of a Cat", "Sibyl", "Spring"
The Pedestal Magazine: "Fear of Snakes"
Poetry Midwest: "Space Journal: The Imaginary Guardian"
Slow Trains: "Fish Dream", "The Garden"
Temeno: "Deconstructing Mahler"
Tipton Poetry Journal: "The Land of Wind"
Umbrella: "Destiny", "Winter Fish"
Visions: "The Emperor's Decree"

Contents

Shard

I let myself fall
I dig with my fingers
into a hole
Mud and gravel fall on my face
The earth closes in on me

I don't stop when my nails break
I miss the sound of birds
I dig toward a hint of light

Each time a new light
strips me naked

Whispers

Alto: seasons. A face with a faint mustache above the firm upper lip.
The scent of ripe fruits and rotten leaves.

Mezzo: crescents. A face brimming with ecliptic dreams.
Dark eyes gather the stars. The scent of lilacs and firewood.

Soprano: sand. A marble face hewed to translucence.
She has entered the gate of childbirth, and become a goddess.

Condensation

An imaginary cat
licks her feet at midnight.

At midnight, the woman
who has been herself all day
(charting the stars,
cooking, doing dishes,
tending to her children)
turns into someone else.

Someone who cannot lower
her gaze from the moon.
Someone who sits in the empty
kitchen, weeping.

One day the cat will materialize.
Everyone will leave her.

Transmutation in the Train

He said his bones were brittle as glass.
He told her he had to be careful.

She said you must be from another planet
on the other side of the Galaxy.

He agreed. She told him she is always right.
He said I am not used to you yet.

Her ears burst with the mews
of her imaginary cat, dying to put
its soft paws on his imaginary cat.

His cat turned into a beagle at the scent
of a new passenger, a tall Ukrainian woman
with pale gray eyes.

Mirages of Indiscretion

The man in a wheelchair contemplated Wagner and the
shrinking death of stars.
Warps in the fabric of space and time.

You contemplate cherry blossoms on my blouse.

The wife conjured Helen and Paris from silenced scripts.
Her lover lit a French cigarette, stood beneath red oaks
outside the house.

*You traveled three continents with a backpack. I dream of women
you assisted.*

The nurse cried watching *Days of Our Lives*, plucked a
rose from the garden.
The man contemplated a white rose in a pink vase.

You quote Nietzsche to mock my theory of the cosmos.

The man divorced his wife of twenty-five years, married
his nurse.
You gave up astronomy in disgust, entered medical school
in a desert.

The Knot

For the last time I imagine
clothing you in black leather
I watch you ride away
on a shining motorcycle
with a woman sitting behind you
Someone you touched when she smiled
hugs tightly to your waist

You touched me when I wept
I saw aurora lit sky
What was your excuse

Someone else sits alone in a gas station
curtained in needles of ice
He draws with his finger on the window
my name in Egyptian hieroglyphs
Your approach rips open
the smooth dance of snow
He puts on a pair of sunglasses
Your girlfriend winks at him
when you turn to pump the gas

Black wings open once
then close for all eternity

To the Alien Listening Through the Galactic Wormhole

Endless bamboo forests breathe
with scarlet orchids.
Will you cross the Galaxy to see
a blue planet waltzing around
a golden star?

Will you ride with the light to hear
sidereal tides rehearse
algae-green incantations
the wind's whisper over
moonlit graveyards?

Will you descend from the invisible
ladder in the sky
to see the prime star vanish?
A blinding diamond ring
encircles the invisible star.

Conception

The unnamed flowers close dead tight. Rain erases a collage
   of footprints.
They wait for ten or twenty years to shed their seeds.

Within a lead sarcophagus, men in Mylar suits search for
   the missing
nuclear fuel that could feed a second chain reaction.

And the aliens, said to be small and with egg size dark eyes,
   could be conducting
biological experiments.

The fire comes. The flowers open again, glow slowly into ashes.
Seeds remain. There will be little parachutes.

Total Solar Eclipse

The black bowl of sky
fills with birds
going home to sleep.

If you seek the sun
you will go blind.

You look down. Your feet
feel the pulsing veins of Earth.

Light begins to spill
from the bottom of sky.
The horizon is dark.
Venus blazes on the white shoulder
of Jupiter.

II

Black Horse

The one-eyed man pulls out a gun, chuckles on-screen. The banker seizes her right hand, hides it between sweaty palms.

> *A fat merchant watched a black horse.*
> *She flew across the prairie in search*
> *of someone else. The silk of her black tail*
> *fought the wind. Sunset dyed the prairie.*

> *Tired of being watched, the horse allowed*
> *the fat man to take her home. He chained her*
> *to a wagon laden with sacks of salt.*

She reads his palms. Credits stream on-screen. She rushes for the door, goes home to map the sky. Constellations barely move in two millennia.

> *She dreams of slender willows in water.*
> *A lanky man in pale silk gazes at her*
> *turns into a crane.*

She once played xiao for a king at dusk. Ruby-throated thrushes answered from bamboos. She studied the moon's tear marks, fingered jade bedrails, considered a scholar who gazed at her and turned away. She wrote poems on white silk, burned them as the king snored.

The scholar avoided her. One day he wandered a secluded path thick with plum petals, eyes half closed. A purple chariot appeared. She stepped down from the chariot, bowed deeply. He blushed. To prove his innocence, he declared women petty creatures, small people without dignity. Two thousand years later she remembers his eyes, drawn back to her as he turned to leave. Two stars refused to dim when the sun whitewashed the sky.

She dreams of a black horse in water.
Her tail spreads into a dark fan.

She screams, wakes to echoes in an empty room. Her window opens to sunlit green peonies. The phone rings. The salt merchant invites her to another movie. She declines, unplugs the phone, tabulates exploding stars.

The rain darkens, reminds her of willows. The scholar has written to request a meeting. She lights a candle, listens to the rain.

The Emperor's Decree

Strangle the Lark.
Place its pink tongue under glass
see what funny mechanism
has made that small creature
a charm in my garden.

Tell the Ladies back
to chambers, and check their own
daydreams: they no longer
need to pose
toward the blooming peach.

Report soon
what you get from the bold Lark
and the curious beauties.
Out! All of you!
Leave me alone.

Damn! The palace is no better
than a luxurious grave
stolen empty by petty robbers.
I shall have someone
cut down that pink tree.

The Elder Beauty

She dreamed of ten cold palaces with ninety-nine beauties in them. The king desired only her. In the peony garden, she swept the wind in a scarlet cape, her son laughing at her side. A white peacock landed on her back, pulled her hair with sharp beak.

At the parade of new conquests, the king dozed on his dragon throne. Moon sat at his feet, voluptuous in a gold brocade gown. He opened his eyes, saw an ultra slender shape departing the royal court. "Hold!" He yelled. "Turn around!" Clad in white silk, the young foreigner had a prominent nose. The king could not withdraw his eyes from her. "I shall call you Willow," the king smiled. Into the tenth cold palace, Moon was ushered.

She dreamed of white haired virgin beauties watching her. Overgrown osmanthus trees shadowed her. Willow gave birth to a boy, who replaced her son as the Crown Prince. She held her son's blood-stained body, cried his name into drifting snow.

Moon bribed her way to see Willow alone, yawning behind beaded curtains. "Sister," she knelt. "I am one of the king's concubines, here to pay my tribute." Willow invited her to play chess. Parakeets lighted on the sunbeam-filled terrace. "Much depends on the pleasure of His Majesty," Willow's voice wavered. Moon nodded, "Sister, no one has pleased His Majesty more. You are perfection, although your nose is a little high." Willow knit her brow. "No worries," Moon smiled. "It can be easily concealed."

She dreamed of leaning against moist railings at dusk. Palace bells chimed. Perfume of white gardenias choked her. She ached for her son, forbidden to her sight. She played meditations on a vertical flute. A star fell from the sky. The flute burst into flames.

The king sent for Moon. "My queen," he said. "I am pestered by a puzzle." She prostrated on the jade floor, spoke with eyes lowered, "If it pleases His Majesty, this worthless slave will swim in boiling oil and die a thousand times." "Hmm," the king continued. "The new beauty seems to cover her nose when I approach her." Moon bowed her head lower. "The humble concubine dares not speak." He frowned. "Speak up and have no fear." She gazed into his eyes. "It has been said that the new beauty cannot stand your celestial scent."

It snowed the next morning. Most unusual for late spring. Peonies drooped in the cold. It was rumored that Willow had been seized for high treason. Her nose was cut off.

Sibyl

I wake from a dream of water's fingernails
scratching limestone boulders
beneath the abandoned temple floor.

My bare feet crush wreaths of gardenias.

Sweet vapor rises from fissures
invisible wrinkles on a stone forehead.
Someone reaches out an alabaster hand
I rise into the air.

The lightning of soft wings.

I advise the King to go east
seek a maiden with a cat's emerald eyes
carry her through a lake of purple lotus.

I pronounce Socrates the wisest of men.

History is the art of revision.
Young priests in white linen tunics
inscribe my predictions in verse.

I blink back voices in the willowy fume.

The tide of mountains will twist and turn.
The scented springs will vanish
erasing traces of faults
converging beneath the temple floor.

Water breathes through my long white hair.

The paths call us with serpentine tongues.
She who leads ascends the blue mountain
overlooking a sea of pink clouds.

Wild Rice

I learned this poem at age twelve:
The humble maiden lives in secret
watches sparrows peck on wild rice
A single stem of nameless weed
blooms in purple clusters

Lanky and nearsighted, I was pushed
by the town's children
as we gleaned in sultry rice fields.
A young peasant gazed into my eyes
as he picked up an armful of rice plants.
He dropped a few stems for me

strutted to the rice-collecting well.
Other peasants glared at him.
He thrashed the rice stalks
against square walls of the well.
Golden grain fell in a sand song.

A young woman had sung the poem
to a famous scholar who pursued her.
As a boy he took buffaloes to swim
in a river littered with duckweed.
She appeared to him in white silk
taught him to read.

An old woman came with a barrel
of bitter tea. I watched him drink.
He squatted on the field's ridge
looked away. I walked the empty field.
Rice stubs jabbed my legs.

The scholar followed her.
She vanished beneath a stone tablet
on the far shore of the river.

The Gift of a Cat

Snow. Everywhere
the whiteness of starlight.
A cat appeared outside my open window
dropped off a parcel
upon our heap of coal.

Stunned by this
I told Mother. She picked it up:
a piece of frozen pork.
Mother cooked it with green chili peppers
and dried wild mushrooms.

That evening by the fire
Father told the story of the poet Li Bai
who declined the Emperor's invitation
until the insolent Prime Minister
came to fetch slippers for him.

I could not stop thinking of the cat
black with green eyes.
Snow filled night with down.
I dreamed of gliding through the emptiness
between the stars.
Their white shadows melted on my skin.
The stars called to me
with the cat's voice.

Space Journal: Passage

I

The ribbon of time stretches
as my ship cuts through black space
nearly catches up with light.
Why do we seek
to prove that we are alone
in this dilute soup of darkness?

I close my eyes, return to myself
at age three. Half-way up the cliff
the silhouette: giant and flower-shaped
herb tree, the untouchable beacon.
White bones scattered in its shadow.
The child I was gazed till her eyes ached
growing more near-sighted.

Mother, the roof is leaking again.
Yellow water rose to tiny ankles.
The child I was, held in the narrow mouth
of a tear in the tableau of space-time.

I turn over in my bunk, hear the child sing:
The mountain is a slumbering horse
Streams course in its heart-caves
You must make water faucets small
Or else two-faced beauty spirits will
stretch out their heads with cloudy hair
to suck in your life-force

The ribbon of time twists
as my ship shakes itself loose
from the tug of invisible tides.

II

Objects form out of nothingness
make space curve around them.
We curve in this curved space.

I close my eyes, hear the thread-thin
voice of myself at age three:
Mother, I had a dream.
Icicles sparkled, laced
the roof of pitch.

In this dream I fly
over double streams lit by rainbows.
I swirl, I glide,
my hair rain of black willow.

Where is my Father?
Mother turned away.

When we look into space
we stare at Time's
blank face, which eats us
digests us
in its expanding sphere.

III

I am a prince in another dream.
On steps of the palace
the maiden sits, a fragile statue.
Her eyes speak to me
of things I do not remember.
I wrap her in my cloak.
The bells ring ceaselessly.

These black bones of Universe
These lonely strings of galaxies
How they glow in hallucination
on the observation screen

Mother, the roof is leaking again.
Mother's tears streamed down the back
of the child I was, trapped in a dimension
that curled into itself.

Do you believe in reincarnation?
The maiden's voice thin, violin-like.
Peoples, streets, canals buried
a thousand feet under the garden.
A man with sapphire eyes
says without moving his lips:
remember your name.

III

Autumn

Autumn is a disease.
Earth's skin sheds
glorious coloration.

Tens of thousands
of wild geese linger at the lake.
They have forsaken long journeys lit by stars.
Their droppings spatter
the narrow wooden bridge.

Blackberries and white daisies
lace the drying bushes.
A broken branch leans into the water.
On the branch green leaves
light the dark satin.
There is no despair without the knowing.

Beneath the sun a sudden blossoming
of peach and pink in distant woods.
Suddenly gone in the wind.

The sun strews golden petals on the water.
Reflected waves smooth incoming waves
into a gilded solid.
Yes, anyone could walk on water
if the purpose became apparent.

The Windowsill

The royal army swarms, charts
a landscape between sharp cliffs
marked by white spirals.
Scouts trace pale green fields
inlaid with blue grass.
A captain discovers warm formations.
They jump.

The astronomer screams, shaking an ant off her hand. The pest-control man puts his elbow on the windowsill, studies the crawling traffic, pours out a small pile of brown grains. She flips through pages of "The Physics of Star Trek." Next morning, the pest-control man puts out a second pile. "They seem to like it," he grins. She puts down her teacup. On the white porcelain, a sage ponders yellow chrysanthemums at sunset.

Brown loaves fall from the sky. The aroma
sweeps workers into frenzy. Some burrow
into the earth with heads and feet, digging tunnels
beneath the palace. Some drag the loaves in teams
of ten. The Queen holds a banquet.
The knights fly about her in ephemeral glory.

The third day only a dozen ants, laden with pale specks, confer on the windowsill. The pest-control man winks through black sunglasses. "We have disturbed the nest. The queen must be dead," he whispers. "They are dividing up the colony and the eggs." She calculates the brightness distribution of 1,000 supernovae. Cosmological standard candles, each brighter than a whole galaxy. Each the explosive death of a star.

The Queen does not wake from sleep.
Her scent chills the palace:
the colony is contaminated. The wind
sent no warning. Several workers grow wings

new Princesses to preside over colonies beyond
the great barrier of weeping willows. We cannot
leave the loaves behind.

*She studies a black and white photo of four astronomers against a
backdrop of the Red Sea. The pest-control man pours out the last
brown grains: "Ground insect, what ants usually eat." A few black
ants lug the grains to a tiny hole in the windowsill's corner. "I am
a vegetarian now," she whispers.*

The Land of Wind

This is a land of spirits.
The wind spreads voices
grains of green sand on red desert.

Those whose land has been stolen
whisper prayers that hover, translating the wind
then rise into a receding cluster of stars.
The wind blows over their graveyard
unmarked, beneath a college town.

Thieves are heroes for their own
children, who pity the native poor
picking through their garbage.
They mow down black locust groves
to build identical houses.

The Universe expands.

The cosmology professor dreams of
being elsewhere.

A spaceship.

View of a dim matrix of lights
each a beating heart and a needle of pain.

The Poet and the Monkey

His wife, a plum tree denying his touch.
He could not bear the glow
of crimson blossoms against a blue sky

above a sea more blue than he thought possible.
Buddha said to the monkey, if you can
traverse my palm in a single somersault

I will set you free.
He loved women so much
gave up his own son for adoption

because the boy was not a girl.
The monkey could cross whole continents
in the flicker of an eyelash. A waterfall concealed

the entrance to his kingdom.
His wife helped him bring from China
a female fan of his poetry. Beneath shadows

of moonlit pines, he slipped into her bed.
His dream of ancient scholarship came true:
plum tree and nightingale, wife and concubine.

He was complete. Poetry flooded. Parades
of beetles. Translucent dreams of hyacinths.
Storms that revived primeval armies

slicing the world with liquid swords.
Death, the ultimate flower
blazed scarlet in a black river.

The monkey found himself in a desert
with a solitary pink obelisk.
The plum tree read the mind

of the nightingale, told her to escape.
The poet loved the pensive bird more than his life.
The monkey shouted for Buddha, the desert

vanished. Buddha held a finger before the monkey.
The poet hacked his wife with an ax
then hung himself from a pine tree.

Crazy Mei

Green rice paddies smell of excrement
masking the scent of yellow rape flowers.
A mud hut roofed by blue tiles
hides in a forest of bamboo.
Mei slouches out of the hut singing
holds a pink plastic bag on her head.

Black clouds rise from distant chimneys
marking red brick highrises.
Mei gazes at the road to the factory.

Once upon a time a factory driver
stopped his truck beside a peasant girl.
A shapely girl whose smile reminded him
of daisies. He took her for a ride
unbuttoned her red blouse
truck in motion. Someone saw them.

The asphalt steams in hot sun.
Mei's eyes grow misty.

A truck appears on the road.
Mei jumps up and down shouting
"Darling, Darling, Wait for Me!"
The driver sees a small red form dashing
toward him. He stamps on the gas pedal.

She clings to the pink plastic bag
printed with the factory's name.
The truck vanishes in a blur.
Mei collapses in its fumes
her red blouse sticks to the black asphalt.

Destiny

Her grandfathers are worshiped in temples
for conquering Nanking in 1937.

She learned at school that the Chinese
invented stories to make the Japanese look bad.

Her mother scrubbed floors on all fours
waiting for her father to return from bars.

She deposited three little prayer tablets
into a stone Buddha, to atone for abortions.

Her boyfriend dreamed of sleeping
with a tall blonde clad in black leather.

She worked several jobs to pay
for a surgeon to stitch back her virginity.

Her parents chose a man their own age.
She wed him in a brocade white gown.

She pretends not to notice her husband's
collection of child pornography.

She teaches her son how to fold a paper
crane, shadow of snow against sunset.

A Water-drop

gathers the world
into its small
naked eye

Space Journal: The Imaginary Guardian

Did you clone me again
from a single strand of black hair?

Shadows of grass stir
over white sand. I hold still
in scorching heat, see time slowing
on the hummingbird's wings.

I curl in the womb drifting
at half the light speed
surrounded by a dark sea of vacuum.

A girl wreathed in purple gardenias
names the leaves of a water oak
after stars in the Milky Way.
A recluse sips blue tea from a clay cup
cross-references poetry spanning
ten thousand years.
A pilot of intergalactic ships
puts her life in your invisible hands.

The womb trembles with my pulse.
Neurons connect, mapping past lives.

The sun swims in ponds:
transient gold fish in land's liquid eyes.
The willow's tender shoots
wrap me in green smoke.

When the womb expels me,
will you receive me with luminous arms?

IV

Letter from Oakland

At noon I close all the windows, draw the curtains.
I shudder when someone walks by outside. Footfalls
ascend the stairs. I close my eyes, see skeletal children
in Ethiopia. Mothers' tears drip into empty straw baskets.

My woman from Andromeda
I want to protect you and our daughter
not yet conceived.

Yesterday the repairman wandered into my room by mistake
found the plant in the closet. Green sawtooth fingers gleamed
under a bare light bulb. My Czech roommate pretended
to know nothing. The repairman declared he stole nothing.

I wish I could see you frown
from your purple planet.

Dark Matter

He dyed his hair green several days before
unusual for a Russian, or a physics graduate student.
No one commented.

Visible: stars, planets, people. Tiny water lilies
in a dark pond. The pond invisible, made of dead stars
black holes, weakly interacting massive particles.

Dark clouds drifted, then dispersed.
The Florida sun came out, blasted its fury.
Vines tangled on banyan trees, rang brilliant yellow bells.
He climbed the stadium's back wall.
His shirt pulled over his head
he hung by his hands.

Deduce the presence of dark matter from movements
of galaxies: the water spins some flowers
tears apart others.

Passersby gathered to watch, saw his legs
tremble a little. They screamed, *Don't Jump.*
He shoved himself away from the wall
into the air
hit a palm tree
then the concrete sidewalk.
The crash set off car alarms.

The Universe may not expand forever.
It may collapse someday, drawn back
by its own dark mass.

The Virgin Beauty at Fifty

She lived in a palace enclosed by peonies and bamboos. A little parrot greeted her each morning: "Good day, young Beauty." The parrot was green as jade. She gazed into the greener pond, pondered shivering reflections.

She entered the royal household at fifteen, one of the chosen maidens to grace the Emperor's bed. She was never sent for. In the first ten years, she plucked strings with snowy fingers each spring night, beneath the moonlit purple magnolia tree. The eunuchs all agreed that she sang like a celestial.

Fallen petals. Fallen leaves. Fallen snow. The cycle repeated. Thirty five years. She only talked to the parrot, never summoned the eunuchs to attend her. They brought her shark fin soup and assorted bean buns on a silver tray, laundered her clothes, swept the yard, watched her feed the parrot from a distance.

One day, trumpets sounded at her door. "Beauty Tang, His Ancient Majesty demands your company," two royal messengers announced in a high pitched smooth tone.

She rouged her face three times, refined her eyebrows with a dark pencil, wrapped herself in bright red satin, as was appropriate for the imperial rendezvous. Eunuchs looked on with tears in their eyes. "Good day, young Beauty." The parrot said. Other beauties watched the procession through gauze curtains.

She never returned. It was said that the young Emperor had dreamed of his father the previous night. The Ancient Emperor told his son that he was lonely in his tomb palace. He wanted the company of one of his Beauties.

Warped Mirrors

The mirror makes Ling's right eyebrow appear higher. She tries to push it lower. Father bangs his fist on the light switch. Beside his drunken red face, the dark length of Mother's tears. Ling remembers crossing a pine forest to seek out the martial arts master. He came out of the two-room hut, frowned. She begged to be his pupil. Tears welled up in her almond eyes. He nodded. She was sixteen, planned to become a master.

> Pursued by the moon's shadowed mirror
> a swan breaks the silence of lilacs

In the backyard yellow chrysanthemums spill over a bamboo fence Mother wove, into the sleepy eye of a black pond. In an art magazine Ling discovers Leda and the Swan. She recalls the poem slipped in under her bolted door, written in bold strokes of an ink-brush. She fled the hut before daybreak, waded through pine needles.

> What is a fish if it does not desire
> the pure depth of a water cavern

Ling takes classes for drawing. Perspectives evade her pencil. She learns tailoring, makes herself fitted shirts from floral crepes. She becomes the town clerk, receives a room, paints orchids and clouds on its white-washed walls. Others toss her name around in the small town, chained to names of boys who help her practice drawing in evenings. She dreams of spring rain.

> What is spring if the earth receives no seeds
> and clouds of dream do not turn to rain

Father empties the liquor bottle into his mouth. He tears off Ling's clothes, makes her kneel before the black pond. He pulls out a bamboo strip from the fence, slashes her snowy back into purple and red stripes. She scratches her face, pounds her head on the ground. A cold wind blows yellow petals in her wet face.

Aspen Trees

sometimes clone themselves. The X chromosome carries a sea of unknown possibilities. O chooses slavery, with whips and branding iron to ensure her never having time to think of men other than her master. He prostitutes her.

Aspen trees are hieroglyphic columns, shaded by tiny throbbing banners of green hearts. The Y chromosome swaps parts with itself, to avoid making everything male. Men rule over women through history. His words, riding crop, and contempt. O considers it her master's godly right to desire other women, helps him trap other women into slavery. She assures him that women are all alike.

Pre-storm wind rushes ten thousand suspended gates of an aspen tree. The Y overwrites itself in some parts, causing male infertility. O's master abandons her. She asks for his permission to die.

Raindrops splash from pale cups of purple-veined morning glories. The Y erodes with time. Men applaud *The Story of O*, written by a woman to impress a man. Women sometimes sleep with men they do not love for conception. Aspen trees shed branches, leaving behind bulging eyes.

Winter Fish

Her screams ran like hunted children crying
"Mother!!!" His fist landed on her face. She stopped
sharp, as if her throat was cut. In the mirror, blood in her
right eye. He told her she imagined it. *Here is what happened.*
He tells her. *A man slaps a woman, and she thanks him.* A black
and white movie he saw. *The quiet gay couple next door, what
they must think. What if they call the police.* She watches the
sun extinguish itself in tall trees. Spring moon hangs low,
a lit fish bowl. Dark tails beat against the glass wall

Seven Days

His hair turned gray overnight. His former students formed gangs, fought each other with knives and rifles. All gangs claimed to be defending Chairman Mao.

He took the train to Beijing. Two days and three nights, he sat in the unswept passenger car, stared through broken windows. Straw huts with doors nailed shut. Vacant factories. Mutilated trees. People foraging in deserted fields. People marching in streets.

In Beijing a distinguished government official listened, offered him top-grade black tea. He bought two jade gauze dresses for his toddler daughters, caught the earliest train home.

His daughters ran to him with shrieks of joy, wrapped their little arms around his legs. His wife turned on the stove to make him noodle soup. Before the water boiled, the door shook. The pretty neighbor next door, a literature teacher who once pursued him, had turned him in to the Red Guards.

A Map of the Universe

A great wall of galaxies spans billions of light years.
A woman searches for planets around other stars.
A man flies an airplane into a skyscraper.

Dark bushes of matter expand
branch off, clump to ignite
star clusters: roses bloom
into an empty Universe.

Brain waves from billions flood a tiny planet.
Chubby teens surf the web for forbidden games.
Skeletal toddlers whimper in fly-infested mud huts.

Naked man and woman twine.
Tinkling pull of dark petals
shapes dreams. Stars hum
from the black rose in the sky.

V

Fear of Snakes

I detour to avoid drowning
in twin tracking mirrors
sunglasses on black-suited businessmen.
I pretend not to see ebony youths
whose sidelong eyes undress me.
Black tulips wither
lead me to a small pond draped
in weeping willows.

A tiny waterlily
breaks the mirror in whiteness.

Please break me
so that I may come back
in a thousand different ways.

Stars embroider a dark void.
I send out a light signal.
It will take four years
for it to reach the nearest star
beyond the Sun.

The Sun will live another 5 billion years.

A warm nudge on my leg
startles me.
A yellow dog dangles his ears
looks at me, rolls in the grass.
Someone whistles.
The dog vanishes faster than the wind.

My long hair winds around my neck.
I tie it into a triple knot.
I dream of looking into the well each night.
The same child sits in the barrel
radiant as the Sun.
The rope slithers through my fingers.
I scream out loud in the birthing room
pulling up the barrel.

Stolen Tears

A moth with goldfish eyes
descends with nightfall.

Light is blotted.
Forest snores.

The magpie robin dreams
of the dinosaur
who invented flight.

The moth inserts a harpoon
under the bird's twin eyelids
drinks tears tasting of the sea.

The magpie robin sleeps
guards the key
to our existence.

Angels in West Virginia

At the hilltop, tiger lilies harvest the searing sun.
She opens the purple velvet bundle for a final look
at her black cat. Another cancer death. The DuPont plant
has thickened the river. She buries her cat in a cypress shade.

Painting: Great Grandmother in a black gown. Hair a burnished red,
right hand reaching out, a gray dove perched on her palm. Mother frowned.
"Granny hated birds." At night she hears gun shots and doors
slammed shut, feels the weight of angels descending through the ceiling.

A dry snake skin hangs from Great Grandfather's headstone.
He fought in the Civil War, fathered a son at sixty. Her Uncle
sat on top of another hill, shot himself in the forehead.
She places a tiger lily on her cat's unmarked grave.

Painting: Blond Grandfather. Blue eyes blaze against starry sky.
He laid railroad tracks in West Virginia. A train carrying fashion shoes
derailed on green mountains. He picked a pair for each lady in the family.
Black shoes for her, ebony as her long straight hair.

She pulls into her garage. The blind old neighbor sits on his porch.
A red pickup truck parks before him. A middle-aged couple
rolls down windows, turns up the car radio's volume, gets out
to sit with the silent old man. After dark a long line of cars
pauses at his house. Bass drums reverberate into the night.

Painting: Dogwoods bent with white blossoms. The morning pale green
turning blue in the distance. She stood before the barrel of a rifle
in Father's hands. He was drunk again. She pushed him back
screamed "Run!" to a squirrel chewing a nut by the road.

An angel smokes a French cigarette, whispers to her through the frosty
glass. She wakes to hear bottles breaking outside her house.
A gray cat licks her feet. She pours bottled water into a bowl for the cat
paints at the easel beneath the dark skylight. A woman stands
in an open field, morphs into a willow. Zebra-striped birds soar overhead.

Daffodils

The bus sped along the rocky road
snaked through sleeping mountains.
The mountains shook their green hair.

An old man in a mud-splashed dark robe
clasped a basket full of golden daffodils.

Men in polyester jackets jammed the aisle
blew cigarette smoke onto my long hair.
A woman shoved through the aisle shouting:
"Show me your ticket, you old thing!"

She grabbed the old man by the shoulder,
"You bought the ticket to Cogongrass Market.
We are now past the Wine Factory!"

Her pimpled face flushed. He trembled.
Eyes of strangers darted away.

My chest stung. My hands searched
my pocket, offered one yuan to the conductor.
She snatched it with a grunt.

Green mountains changed into bald hills
lit at night by green fires
from mounds of moist earth.

"Tomb Fields," the conductor yelled.
The old man looked at me, stepped out
into the graveyard. His daffodils
cupped the slant afternoon sun.

Father Sleeping

"If you really don't want to go, you won't have to…" Father's voice swam, a carp in the muddy water of summer afternoon. I tiptoed to the living room, saw Father's belly rise and fall. His hair, white grass against the paisley sofa. His face calm and agitated at once. A fish caught in its own shadow.

The night before, he asked me to visit peasant cousins I barely knew. I refused. Father's face reddened under the bare light bulb. He walked away slowly, careful not to erase the map he drew in chalk on the concrete floor, marking all the places I ought to see. Three Gorges. Tibet. Some distant Palace. A temple with rare stone tablets of calligraphy.

I picked up a comb from the table. It stuck in my tangles of long hair. Through the door I saw Mother in the itchen, shredding blurred zucchini for supper. She had lost one eye in an operation. The doctor thought she had cancer.

Father sneered when Mother tripped over things. A caged cat watching a half-blind mouse. Mother believed in Chairman Mao once. She handed Father's diaries to Red Guards. Father fumed when Mother tried to sue a student of his for hitting her in the eye. "It was a gang fight," Father whispered to me. "How could she tell who hit her."

Father stopped mumbling, started to snore. My cheeks and neck were wet. "You are my only friend," Father had told me. His best friend died, Father sat fishing on the riverbank each day. Mountains of shadows drifted before him.

I cupped the light bulb with my hand. Softly, Mother called my name from another room.

The Aggregate of Routines

The sea sweeps up in white-lace trim
teases the land.

Starlings swarm into the air:
a twisting stair of black velvet.

Someone set fire to forests in Australia.
People burned to death in their cars.

I shut off the radio
try to remember the dolphins.

The sea: fluidity of sleep.

Twilight waves polish
the mirror of sand.

Someone wore explosives under an abaya
entered a tent full of women and children.

I shut off the television
try to count tiny green tea leaves.

The sea erodes the land.
The land sips the sea.

Dark waves pulse
against a veil of starlight.

I ride a lone dolphin
away from the invisible shore.

Dreamscape

Mad men were counting down
to detonate the planet.
Dreams directed us to
Tunnel Number Two beneath the sea.

On the other side: a land of white
lotus.
We learned to live without eating.

We conversed in poetry.

The explosion carried our oxygen
iron, magnesium
into opaque
intergalactic clouds.

We grew translucent wings.

Thanksgiving

A woman with a painted face and
a pig's body, wrapped in pastel knit.
Beside her, a man in a black suit
and a tall hat.
I wake up shaking. Outside
darkness wails.

Mama, but how do we get a turkey
to jump into the oven?

We stand in line for vaccination
against the swine flu.
The woman and pig hybrid
plays shadow with my breath.

Mama, will we be extinct
like the Tyrannosauruses?

Riverbed pebbles remember
the ocean's salty taste.
I will hear the flute call
languidly. My ashes will embrace
an estranged star. My son
will open his hands to let go
moisture fogging his space-visor.

Some dinosaurs became eagles.
A circle has no sides.

Alex the gray parrot said, *I love you,*
be good. Oceans will rise and fall. Someone
will decipher the pigs' language.

Space Journal: Time Machine

A hundred red lanterns haunt the banquet.
glow with hieroglyphic poems.
A Chinese businessman pours Maotai
into a child-shaped ivory cup to thank me.
I designed his satellite network, cannot touch
the cup. Men in metallic suits clamor for me
to drink. I speak in Chinese about my wife.
How she pulls on a black leather hood
to spy on criminals in the Market Place.
Their laughter deflates the lanterns.

     *   *   *

I pose for a sculptor in Rome.
He pulls down my blue silk robe
accuses me of changing into a woman.
I look down at my chest and see
twin mountains on a flat landscape.
Wind descends from the chapel ceiling
where God reaches out a finger to Adam
from a human-brain shaped cloud.
The sculptor shoves me out into the street
curses, slams the door.

     *   *   *

Morning opens: a flower unfurls petals of light.
I step out from the waterfall.
Window-size bubbles drift close overhead.
Each contains a new destination.

VI

Meditation on Hair

A school of fish enters the dark cove
races for pulsing cocoons. Live scripts
of intricate twists and turns.

You ponder the origin of arrows.
Eyes of strangers swim
the dark waterfall of your hair.

Time erodes you
into the ambience of hyacinth.
You read yourself from cover to cover.

A single fish survives, decoded
to form a new universe.
Your hair never reaches your ankles

its length cannot exceed the lifespan
of a single hair. You arrange tea leaves
into patterns of Cygnus and Orion

dream of slender men in a starlit forest
metamorphosing into swans that glow
in flight into a liquid sky.

You are a room that grows with its occupant
tapping your insides with tiny feet and fists.
You are a room filled with iridescent echoes.

Nascent shoots bristle on the horizon.
The drummer squeezes through
the tunnel to dry, airy light.

Time erodes you. Hummingbirds flee.
A glistening in the mirror: needles of white hair.
The roots within your head discuss your change.

Finally, you enter a lake of indigo stars.
Your hair continues to grow beneath the earth
until your body dissolves in fossils' exhalations.

Echoes of Trees on the Mountaintop

It started with echoes in the dark hall.
I floated on waves of Father's baritone
in the boat that was his arms.

I had measles, screamed.
Father carried me off at midnight
rocked me, chanted poems.

I grew up dreaming of drunken poets
heroes who died laughing
ruined palaces, the distant sea.

I squinted to see things.
To cure it Mother fed me shark liver pills
made me sit outside on a tall stool
to count trees on the Mountain.

I knew all the trees on the Mountain.
A king and three daughters. Warriors in armor.
Blind beggars standing with one leg.

The teachers' handwriting on the blackboard
shimmers of silver fish in a dark pool.
I squinted more. No one noticed.

Mother was ashamed of Father
locked up for what he had written.

Called many names by the other children
I stopped counting the trees, hid
in dark corners to read books.

Deconstructing Mahler

Would Gustav Mahler go skiing?
Would I stop my imaginary cat from following
a thin stranger who teased me
with quotations from Nietzsche?

Water drops gather in the air
at the right place and right time:
a rainbow.

Mahler became a Catholic
so that he could direct the Vienna Opera
own a grand villa by the lake in Carinthia.
Did Hitler know that Mahler was a Jew?
Ashes snowed over Auschwitz.

Water covered earthquake:
a tsunami.

Mahler's first born died at age five.
He composed his last
unfinished symphony
while his wife dallied with another man.

The ocean gives life.
The ocean cries.
The ocean absorbs.
The ocean laughs.

Someone dons a sky blue ski suit
rides his motorcycle against snow mountains
white as elephants.

I enter motherhood.
Green flash over the ocean:
a symphony of anonymous water drops.

Mahler rises out of dark blue waves.
His fifth symphony tinges the air with
deep purple.
My imaginary cat glides into the air.

Spring

Broken cobwebs stream in the sun, mark
temperament of the wind.
Blackbirds rise from a silver landscape.

"You must kneel," said the Buddhist nun.
She struck the bells before each
of three shrines
chanted in southwestern Chinese.
The incense sparked.

A new world has begun.
Its beacon throbs within my belly.

     *   *   *

Rain strings echoes of night.
Regurgitated sunlight flows in veins
within naked brown bark
suddenly bursts
into plum blossoms.

The liquid universe expands.
Its inhabitant discovers dream.

     *   *   *

Eagles' wings brush the wind.
The wind brushes the eagles' shadows
off newly green tree tops.

The river's sun scales
weave from past to future.

I watch the black and white screen
as you deliver a power kick
to the sonic probe.
Your silent laughter ripples
through the moonscape
inside my belly.

Adagio

Yellow silver fish sparkle
near the pond's bottom.
You count them
feel their tails brushing
gently against your thighs.

Your body remembers.
Stray light on a black river
floating shadows of swans.

Touch the fish without
disturbing their course.
They are leaving
water, to swim in air.

Fishtails electrify your fingertips.
You feel the storm coming.

Fish Dream

Against the glass, whirled reflections of a green humming-bird. The sun warms red nectar in the lantern-shaped feeder. Four times farther out than the Earth, Jupiter orbits the Sun with its entourage of moons.

A six pound carp leaped into my lap, its round mouth reached for my breasts. I jumped, saw a black pond in which galaxies swim. Two young galaxies brushed shoulders. Each grew arms, spirals of blue and white stars.

The hummingbird enters the open glass door, pecks the white wall, then another white wall. His intermittent swirls echo in the room. "Feel the wind," I tell him. He dashes to the corner, disappears behind an unused screen. I lift the screen. He is frozen, with one wing folded.

My baby puckers up in his sleep, suckles on moist air tinted with magnolia.

In a quantum foam of fluctuating space and time, the Universe was born. Our minds peck against walls of unknown thickness. In a Pakistani mountain's dark belly, a mad man nourished by tribal deliveries plots the destruction of innocent millions. On an icy moon of Jupiter, evolution awaits.

Baby in one arm, I scoop up the hummingbird with my other hand. He is motionless, warm. I step outside the door, open my hand: he soars into the sky in an emerald flash.

The Web

Fragments of insects
hang from tenuous threads.

A girl is raped, murdered, mutilated.
She speaks from heaven in a novel.
A young man who aspires
to jihad, assaults bloggers
who favor exploration of the Universe.

Beads of darkness absorb slivers
of starlight. Weaving.

The wind snickers. Snow withdraws
the dance of a thousand veils
high above the tree line.
A little pig ponders the geometry
of Cygnus.

Hidden in rain forest roots:
translucent orchids, each smaller
than a teardrop.

The Garden

Wind whips air into snowflakes.
The mind rises, buoyant
over skeletal crystals.
I reach out my hands.
The stars listen.

In this scenario I explore
the physiology of wings. They begin
to grow on my back ribs.
I try not to scratch.
The current of time slows, loops into a pond.
I look into the water's black mirror, see
weeping cherry blossoms.

Light floods. Naked limbs of white maples
stretch into an eggshell sky.

Buffalo Point

Water drops tumble down the skirt
of stone
into a green pool
reflecting gold-veined bluffs

A pale-tailed fish circles
close to surface
jumps at the splashing from a rock
tossed by a boy

Wind sighs through bamboo leaves
pauses at white plum blossoms
hanging over the cliff

A small cave forms a room
Arched ceiling bends in petals
of a single lotus flower
The back window opens into receding
smaller rooms
No end in sight

The boy can sense the bats

Somewhere underground
twenty two stories deep
dark echoes explore the intention
of wet limestone
It grows a translucent universe
One inch per century

Futurescape

Thunder of applause
followed by rain on the desert.
A single yellow flower
opens from a cactus palm.

A child sleeps.
Oars navigate an opal sea.

The Sun will die in five billion years.
Ten million spaceships will depart
from its white dwarf corpse.

A kiss sparks
beneath a canopy of cherry blossoms.
Electricity of one thousand faces
carved in breathing stone
rushes from Notre Dame.

Protons will decay.
The Universe will dissipate
back into a sea
of space-time foam.

Child, you are the guide
in my journey. I climb on
the boat of your laughter.

VII

Three Lotus Ponds

A boy had three lotus ponds:
sky blue bloomed in one, sunrise pink in another
ivory white in the third.

He had three palaces: one for the cold
season, another for the hot season, another
for the rainy months. Leaning on carved
sandalwood panels, he listened to musicians
starry-eyed women plucking strings.
Their slender white fingers shone in the mist.

One day, he left the palace for a walk.
He saw a wailing crowd by the Ganges
a corpse on a funeral pyre.
As it burned he felt the change within him.

Years later
a bowl of water became the ocean.
He became the Buddha.

Prescience

I am afraid to write for you.
Fear that the lure of poetry's dark corridors
will foreshadow your life.
Fear that plain good wishes
(such as those versed by Su Dong-Po
for his infant son)
will tempt Fate to contradiction.

A matrix of fish leaps for the moon.
The sea sends signals through the air.
Someone searches for the signature
of water
beyond the veil of stars.

You have climbed ashore from my dream.
Pushing your tiny feet against my lap
you try to stand up.

Evolution

A greedy merchant in China substituted powdered sugar
for baby formula. Thirty thousand infants
died of malnutrition.

She became a vegetarian after reading
an American professor's review of cannibalism
in Chinese literature. It elaborated on a novel
by a man about auctioning off a mother
and her child, with the crowd
debating their qualities as meat.

In the jungle each mother breast-feeds her young
to avoid predators tracking them
through the smell of tiny feces.

Three miscarriages followed in two years.
At the first sign of this baby she resumed eating
chicken, lit incense in a Buddhist temple.
She dreams of humans evolving into
beings with no need to eat living things.
The baby cries. Her breasts become fountains of milk.

The future beings thrive on sunlight.
Her ears tingle from
the music of their luminous green wings.

Dark Energy

Mayan nobles sometimes marched their children
on winding paths up snow mountains.
They would dig a square room, light a fire
leave the children with jugs of elixir
prepared by the priests.

The children sang softly, drank, slept
never woke.
The gods did not come.

The Universe is mostly empty.
Space expands. Galaxies drift away
from each other at accelerated speeds.

Perhaps only the priests
led the children on their last journey.
If the gods had been watching, they would have
knocked the cups from the little hands
carried the children into their beryllium chariot
beamed the priests into the ice-hidden tomb —
at least for a few hours.

Child, look for others
in the Milky Way's outskirts.
Someday you will return my ashes
to the stars. You will ponder
pathways to other universes.

Photo by Pia Mukherjee

YUN WANG was born and grew up in southwest China. Her poetry book, *The Book of Jade*, won the Nicholas Roerich Poetry Prize from Story Line Press and was published in 2002. Her poetry chapbook, *The Carp*, was published by Bull Thistle Press in 1994. She has published poems and translations of classical Chinese poetry in numerous literary journals. Wang has been a professor of Physics and Astronomy at the University of Oklahoma since 2000, and a Senior Research Scientist at California Institute of Technology since 2015. Wang is a cosmologist, and the author of the technical book, *Dark Energy*, published by Wiley-VCH in 2010.